June 2004

Berlin, city of Action, "with it" in the world, Awake, New + Old working Together People, civilized, Dynamic Sidewalk cafes + OH what Great Pilsners + a Million Mercedes Benzs without one Scratch!

If you where here with me I would have Loved it even More

Because we Belong + enjoy the Moments Together!

Love
Gary

Berlin Panorama einer Stadt
Panorama of a City

Berlin Panorama einer Stadt
Panorama of a City

Fotografien von Carl-Heinz Hatebur

nicolai

Vorwort

Der Faszination Berlins bin ich bereits bei meinem ersten Aufenthalt in dieser Stadt im Frühjahr 1979 erlegen – und sie hat seither nicht nachgelassen. Für mich ist es eine herrliche, schöne und auf liebenswerte Weise verrückte Stadt. Mit Menschen, die sich gerne ins Gespräch ziehen lassen, die bei aller Bissigkeit doch oft bereit sind, lächelnd einen völlig anderen Standpunkt zu akzeptieren. Es ist kaum möglich, sich an Berlin satt zu sehen: nicht nur, weil die Stadt in ständiger Bewegung ist, sich unaufhörlich verändert, sondern auch weil das bereits Bestehende und Bekannte immer neue Aspekte bietet, sich oft auf nicht vorhersehbare Weise ins Ganze einfügt. Der fotografische Blick auf Berlin, der Versuch, mit der Kamera Perspektiven zu eröffnen und Strukturen zu Tage treten zu lassen, Einblicke und Einsichten zu verschaffen – das ist meine Methode, der besonderen Faszination Berlins nachzuspüren und für mich und andere ins Bild zu setzen.

Foreword

As long ago as the first time I stayed in Berlin, in the spring of 1979, I succumbed to the fascination exercised by this city – and the strength of the feeling has continued unabated to the present day. I experience it as a gloriously beautiful and at the same time delightfully crazy city – one where people are altogether willing to be drawn into conversation, and are often prepared, for all their acerbity, to accept with a smile a point of view quite opposed to their own. It is hardly possible to have one's fill of looking at Berlin: not just because the city is in a state of perpetual motion and subject to incessant change, but also because its constant and familiar features are always presenting new aspects, finding a place for themselves in the whole that is often quite unforeseen. To create a view of Berlin in photographs, to try to open up its perspectives with the camera, to cast light upon its structures, to create insights and realisations – this has been my chosen method of pursuing the special fascination of the city

Die Blickwinkel, aus denen die Fotografien in diesem Buch aufgenommen wurden, entsprechen zwei grundlegenden Bedürfnissen: dem, Distanz zu schaffen und Übersicht zu gewinnen, und dem, sich unter die Bewohner der Stadt zu mischen, die Nähe zu den Berlinern zu suchen. Für beide Anliegen erwies sich die Panoramakamera als das geeignete Instrument. Eine Fotografie zeigt immer nur einen Ausschnitt der Realität. Das kann als Möglichkeit zum gestaltenden Eingriff in die Welt verstanden werden, ist zugleich aber auch stets eine Begrenzung der eigenen Sicht. Die Panoramakamera vermag zumindest in subjektiver Hinsicht diese Begrenzung zu überwinden. Sie funktioniert ähnlich wie das menschliche Auge, indem das Objektiv horizontal wandert; außerdem hat sie einen Blickwinkel, der dem des Menschen gleicht, nämlich 135 Grad. Andere Gegebenheiten rücken dadurch in den Blick: die Dimensionen von Gebäuden, die Ausdehnung von Flächen, der Verlauf von Sichtachsen, urbane Konstellationen und Zusammenhänge, die Bedeutung der Wasserwege für das Stadtbild und nicht zuletzt der Himmel, der Himmel über Berlin. Die ganze Stadt wird als Landschaft sichtbar, nicht erst dort, wo sie wie im Berliner Westen tatsächlich in eine parkähnliche Landschaftsszenerie übergeht.

and putting it into the picture for myself and for others.
The visual angles from which the photographs in this book were taken were based on two fundamental requirements: on the one hand that of creating distance and attaining to an overview, on the other that of mingling with the inhabitants of the city, of coming to close quarters with the people of Berlin. For both aspirations the panoramic camera proved to be the most suitable instrument.
A photo invariably shows just a section of reality. We can understand this as giving us the opportunity of shaping and engaging with the world, but at the same time it is bound to be a limitation of one's own vision. The panoramic camera can overcome this limitation, from a subjective point of view at any rate. It functions in a way similar to the human eye, in that the lens moves in a horizontal direction; and moreover its angle of vision is similar to that of a human being, namely 135 degrees. As a result other realities come into view: the dimensions of buildings, the extension of open spaces, the path followed by the axis of sight, urban constellations and connections, the significance of the waterways for shaping the image of the city and also, last but not least, the sky, the sky above Berlin. The city becomes visible as a

Die städtebauliche Anlage Berlins kommt dieser Sichtweise allerdings auch sehr entgegen. Mit seinen langen Straßen, breiten Boulevards und ausgedehnten Parkanlagen, mit der gesetzlichen Festlegung der Traufhöhe, die in weiten Bereichen ein einheitliches Stadtbild bewahrt hat (die markanteste Ausnahme bildet der Potsdamer Platz), bietet sich Berlin – anders als vertikal ausgerichtete Großstädte wie zum Beispiel New York oder Frankfurt am Main – geradezu an, in Panoramen vorgestellt zu werden. Diese Rundblicke habe ich in Farbe aufgenommen, das entspricht meines Erachtens einer klassischen Sichtweise, die immer auch Glanz und Pracht einer Stadt enthüllen soll.

Eine Art Kontrapunkt zu den weiten Perspektiven der Farbaufnahmen bilden die Schwarz-Weiß-Bilder. Hier ging es mir darum, die Menschen in Berlin zu zeigen – wie es ihnen gelingt, die Enge in einer Großstadt zu ertragen oder auch, was durchaus vorkommt, zu genießen. Ich bin ihnen auf den Straßen und in Parks, in Kneipen, Cafés und Museen begegnet, habe sie im vertrauten Gespräch, beim Spiel, in öffentlichen Versammlungen oder in stiller Betrachtung von Kunstwerken beobachtet. Die Schwarz-Weiß-Fotografien leben vor allem von der Reduktion auf Blick, Mimik und Gebärde, Farbe würde hier nur ablenken. So richtet

landscape in its entirety – not just at that point in West Berlin where it does indeed merge into the scenery of a landscape resembling a park. It must be said that Berlin lends itself eminently to this mode of vision, in consequence of the way the city is laid out. With its long streets, broad boulevards and extensive parks, with the statutory prescription of the height of the eaves of a house, which has maintained a consistent image over a great part of the city (the most striking exception being the *Potsdamer Platz*), Berlin lends itself in the highest degree – by contrast with vertically conceived cities like New York or Frankfurt am Main for instance – to a panoramic presentation. I have taken these panoramic shots in colour: this, in my view, is in keeping with a classical mode of vision, which should always reveal the brilliance and splendour of a city.

The black and white pictures form a kind of counterpoint to the extended perspectives of the coloured photographs. Here my objective was to show the people living in Berlin – to show how they succeed in coping with the confinement of living in the big city, or even (for this too is perfectly possible) enjoying it. I have met them on the streets and in parks, in bars, cafés and museums; I have observed them in intimate dialogue, at play, at public meetings

sich die Aufmerksamkeit auf die Großstädter in ihrem Miteinander oder auch ihrem Gegeneinander, ihre verschiedenen Kommunikationsweisen kommen zum Ausdruck. Das urbane Leben offenbart sich als ein dichtes, in ständiger Bewegung befindendes Geflecht von Mitteilungen. Auch dafür ist die Panoramakamera hervorragend geeignet; sie muss sich, wenn man nahe an die Menschen herangeht, nicht auf Einzelne beschränken, sie fixiert keine isolierten Handlungen, sondern erfasst Gruppen in ihrer Dynamik. Die Reaktionen der Fotografierten war übrigens höchst unterschiedlich; gemeinsam aber war ihnen, dass sie durchweg positiv ausfielen und ich stets auf Verständnis traf, häufig sogar spürte, dass die Fotografierten stolz und geschmeichelt waren, wenn ich ihnen erklärte: »Ich fotografiere das Berliner Leben, das Leben in Berlin.«

Wer den Überblick gewinnen will, muss hoch hinaus – in einer Stadt wie Berlin ist das nicht ohne Anstrengung und manchmal nur mit beträchtlichem Aufwand möglich. Zu den Zeiten, als Berlin noch geteilt war, gab es weitere Herausforderungen. Mich interessierten damals die alten Sichtachsen der Stadt, die durch die Mauer unterbrochen waren. Wenn ich die Leiter an die Mauer stellte, um eine West-Berliner Sichtachse in den Osten zu verlängern, konnte

or when engaged in the quiet contemplation of works of art.

These black and white photos draw their power above all from the reduction of the subject to looks, gestures and attitudes. Colour would only be a distraction here. So the attention is drawn to the inhabitants of the city in their togetherness, or for that matter in situations of opposition, enabling their various styles of communication to find expression. Urban life reveals itself to be a densely packed web of communication which is never still for a moment. The panoramic camera is admirably suited to this as well: in a close approach to the human subject it does not have to limit itself to individual details, it does not fix on an isolated activity, but embraces the group as a dynamic entity. The reactions of the people I photographed were exceedingly varied, by the way; all the same, there was a feature common to them all, namely that the encounters always had a positive note and people were invariably understanding, so that I frequently sensed, even, that they were proud to be photographed, and felt themselves flattered when I told them, "I am photographing Berlin life, life in Berlin."

If you want to get an overview, you need to ascend to a height. In a city like Berlin this is not possible without exertion, and sometimes

ich sicher sein, dass es bald sehr lebendig auf dem »Todesstreifen« wurde: Cabriotrabbis kamen gefahren, Feldtelefone wurden gekurbelt, Ferngläser blitzten, die geballte Aufmerksamkeit der Grenzwächter konzentrierte sich auf mich.

Zwei Gebäude spielten für die Farbaufnahmen in diesem Band eine wichtige Rolle, weil sie einen weiten Blick auf Berlin gestatten: die Gedächtniskirche und der Berliner Dom. Ich hatte immer schon davon geträumt, das Kreuz auf dem Glockenturm zusammen mit dem »hohlen Zahn« optisch knapp über den Horizont des Kurfürstendamms zu setzen. Nachdem ich von der zuständigen Pastorin das Einverständnis erhalten hatte, zog ich eine dreiteilige Bocksleiter auf den zweiundsechzig Meter hohen Glockenturm, zurrte dieses sechsmeterachtzig hohe »Stativ« am Rande des Turmes fest, stellte mich, zitternd vor Angst, rücklings auf die fünftletzte Sprosse, griff ganz langsam nach meiner Kamera und genoss minutenlang eine einzigartige Perspektive, die Erfüllung eines lang gehegten Traums. Die Leiter blieb wochenlang auf dem Glockenturm, bis ich alle meine Bilder gemacht hatte.

Der Berliner Dom ist in der Mitte der Stadt eine Art Dreh- und Angelpunkt. Nachdem ich den Dombaumeister sechs Monate vergeblich mit

can be managed only with considerable efforts. In the epoch when Berlin was still a divided city there were further challenges. It was the city's old axes of sight, interrupted by the Wall, that interested me in those days. If I propped my ladder against the Wall, so as to extend a West Berlin axis of sight in an easterly direction, I could be confident that there would soon be lively activity in the "forbidden zone": open-top Trabbis would drive up, field telephones would be activated, binoculars flash, and the full concentrated attention of the border guards be focussed on me.

Two buildings had an important part to play in connection with the colour photographs in this volume, as giving an extended view over Berlin. These were the *Gedächtniskirche* [Kaiser Wilhelm Memorial Church] and the *Berliner Dom*. I had always dreamed of placing the cross on the bell-tower along with the "hollow tooth" of the church optically just above the horizon of the *Kurfürstendamm*. After obtaining permission from the lady minister responsible, I hauled a three-section stepladder onto the 62-metre-high bell-tower, lashed this 6.8-metre-high "tripod" firmly to the side of the tower, positioned myself, shaking with terror, on the fifth from highest rung, facing backwards, and slowly, very slowly reached for my camera. For some

Blick auf dieses Buchprojekt umworben hatte, brachten schließlich die in der Zwischenzeit entstandenen Bilder, die ich ihm zeigte, die Wende: Ich durfte meine Leiter über die Wendeltreppe auf den Turmrundgang bugsieren, und dann war es wieder da, dieses Staunen. Es ist ein erhebendes Glücksgefühl, wenn eine Aufnahme, die schon lange in der Phantasie lebte, sich als realisierbar zeigt. Monate später an einem Wintertag brach die untergehende Sonne unter der Wolkendecke durch, und ich wusste: Das ist mein Bild.

Bei den Kranführern, die ich ebenfalls oft um Hilfe bat, gab es ein sicheres Mittel, sie gewogen zu stimmen: einen Kasten Bier. Hatte man in dieser Währung bezahlt, gaben sie mit einem breiten Grinsen ihr Okay. Als ich in der Oranienburger Straße auf einem Kran stand, um die Neue Synagoge zu fotografieren, hörte ich plötzlich dumpfe Schläge, und als ich hinunter sah, stellte ich fest, dass die Monteure bereits begonnen hatten, den Kran zu demontieren. Wieder musste der gewohnte Obolus entrichtet werden, damit mir die Männer die halbe Stunde schenkten, die ich brauchte, um die Synagoge aufs Bild zu bannen. Manches wurde sehr viel einfacher, als ich mich an eine Firma für hydraulische Arbeitsbühnen wandte und dort ein offenes Ohr für mein Anliegen fand. Mit diesen

minutes I enjoyed a unique perspective – the fulfilment of a long cherished dream. The ladder stayed on the bell-tower for weeks, until I had taken all the pictures I needed.

The *Berliner Dom* is a kind of hinge and pivot at the heart of the city. After I had vainly wooed the works manager for six months in connection with the project of this book, when at last I showed him the pictures I had taken in the mean time, this finally tipped the scales: I was granted permission to manoeuvre my ladder up the spiral staircase onto the walkway that goes around the tower, and there it was again – the same breathless amazement. It is uplifting, and causes a feeling of great happiness, when it proves possible to realise a photo that has had a life of its own in your imagination for years. Months later, on a winter day, the sinking sun broke through under a canopy of cloud, and I knew – That is the picture I want.

As for the crane drivers, on whose help I was also frequently dependent, there was a reliable method of obtaining their goodwill: it just took a crate of beer. If payment had been made in this currency, they would grin broadly and tell me to go ahead. Once when I was standing on a crane in the *Oranienburger Strasse*, trying to get a photo of the *Neue Synagoge*, I suddenly heard muffled thumps and saw, looking down,

Bühnen konnte ich fast beliebig meine strategischen Punkte im Koordinatennetz dieser Stadt besetzen.

Die Auswahl der Bilder in diesem Buch ist, wie kann es anders sein, subjektiv. Die wichtigen Sehenswürdigkeiten dieser Stadt, die Magneten des Publikumsinteresses, sind vertreten. Daneben aber gibt es auch Blicke auf weniger bekannte Orte und auf den vielfältigen Alltag in Berlin – Ansichten und Atmosphären, die für mich ebenso stark die Physiognomie dieser Stadt prägen. Vieles wird, schon aufgrund des besonderen, schwer zugänglichen Standortes, den ich häufig gewählt habe, ungewohnt erscheinen. Ich sehe dies als meinen Beitrag zu dem Facettenreichtum, zur Faszination Berlins.

Carl-Heinz Hatebur

that the mechanics had already started to take down the crane. Again I had to pay in the customary coinage to persuade the men to give me the half-hour that I needed in order to conjure the synagogue into a picture. A great many things became a lot easier after I addressed myself to a firm specialising in hydraulic working platforms, and found that they were prepared to lend an ear to my request. Using these platforms, I was able to occupy just about any of my strategic points in the network of coordinates that makes up the city.

The selection of pictures in the book is subjective – as is inevitable. The important tourist attractions of the city, the magnets that draw the attention of the general public, have been covered. Alongside these, though, there are also glimpses of localities that are less well known, and of the multifarious daily life of Berlin – views and atmospheres which to my mind are just as important in the way they characterise the physiognomy of this city. Much in this book will appear unusual, just in view of the barely accessible standpoint that I frequently chose. I see it as being my contribution to this richly many-faceted city, to the fascination of Berlin.

Carl-Heinz Hatebur

Danken möchte ich in besonderem Maße meiner Frau Tina Hatebur für ihre Geduld und Herrn Behrmann von der Firma Easy Lift für die gewährte Unterstützung. Der Pastorin Frau von Kekulé und dem Dombaumeister Herrn Hoth danke ich für ihre Hilfe.

Geleitet hat mich bei der Arbeit an diesem Buch das Motiv »Suchet der Stadt Bestes« (Jeremia 29.7).

I particularly wish to thank my wife Tina Hatebur for her patience and Mr. Behrmann from the company Easy Lift for the support granted. Furthermore, I sincerely thank vicar Mrs. von Kekulé and the Dombaumeister Mr. Hoth for their help.

My work on this book was guided by the motive from Jeremiah 29,7 "... and seek the peace of the city".

Panoramen
Panoramic views

Pariser Platz mit Brandenburger Tor; rechts das Gebäude der Französischen Botschaft

Pariser Platz with Brandenburg Gate; on the right the French embassy building

vorhergehende Seite:
Pferde bändigende Dioskuren (im Vordergrund und rechts) auf der Kuppelummantelung des Alten Museums; links der Berliner Dom

previous page:
Dioscuri taming horses (in the foreground and on the right) on the cupola surround of the *Altes Museum*; *Berliner Dom* on left

Reichstagsgebäude, Sitz des Bundestages; im Vordergrund eine der Rotunden des Paul-Löbe-Hauses

Reichstag building, the seat of the federal parliament; in the foreground one of the rotundas of the Paul Löbe building

Im Inneren der Glaskuppel des
Reichstagsgebäudes

In the interior of the glass cupola
of the *Reichstag* building

vorhergehende Seite:
Blick vom Dach der Schweizer
Botschaft auf Bundeskanzleramt
(rechts) sowie Reichstag und
Paul-Löbe-Haus (links)

previous page:
View from the roof of the Swiss
embassy towards the office of
the Federal Chancellor (right);
Reichstag and Paul Löbe building can also be seen (left)

Schloss Bellevue, Amtssitz
des Bundespräsidenten

Schloss Bellevue, official seat
of the Federal President

Lichthof mit Galerien im Bundespräsidialamt, Tiergarten

Internal glass-roofed courtyard with galleries in the Office of the Federal President; *Tiergarten*

Empfang des nigerianischen Präsidenten im Ehrenhof von Schloss Bellevue

The Nigerian president being welcomed on the ceremonial courtyard of Schloss Bellevue

Das Ensemble der Nordischen Botschaften am Klingelhöferdreieck am südlichen Rand des Tiergartens

The group of Scandinavian embassies on the *Klingelhöferdreieck* on the southern side of the *Tiergarten*

Fassade der mexikanischen Botschaft am Klingelhöferdreieck

Façade of the Mexican embassy on the *Klingelhöferdreieck*

Im Innenhof des Hauses der Deutschen Industrie in der Breite Straße in Mitte

In the interior courtyard of the *Haus der Deutschen Industrie* (House of German Industry) in the *Breite Strasse* in *Mitte*

vorhergehende Seite:
Potsdamer Platz

previous page:
Potsdamer Platz

Empfang in der Schweizer Botschaft

Reception at the Swiss Embassy

Die DaimlerChrysler-City am Potsdamer Platz mit dem Hochhausturm der debis-Zentrale am Landwehrkanal

The DaimlerChrysler City on the *Potsdamer Platz* with the high-rise tower of the debis headquarters on the *Landwehrkanal*

Die Philharmonie (links), der Kammermusiksaal und die Sankt-Matthäus-Kirche am Kulturforum

The Philharmonic hall (left), the chamber music concert hall and the Church of St. Matthew on the *Kulturforum*

Im Café Tucher am Pariser Platz   In the *Café Tucher* on the *Pariser Platz*

Am Neuen See im Tiergarten   By the *Neuer See* in the *Tiergarten*

Neue Nationalgalerie (links) und Staatsbibliothek (Mitte); im Hintergrund rechts das debis-Hochhaus

New *Nationalgalerie* (left) and *Staatsbibliothek* (centre); in the background, on right, the debis high-rise building

Die Siegessäule am Großen Stern im Tiergarten

The victory pillar on the *Grosser Stern* in the *Tiergarten*

Picknick im Tiergarten   Picnic in the *Tiergarten*

Am Großen Stern im Tiergarten während der Love Parade

On the *Grosser Stern* in the *Tiergarten* during the Love Parade

Haus der Kulturen der Welt (ehemals Kongresshalle) im Tiergarten

Haus der Kulturen der Welt (formerly the *Kongresshalle*) in the *Tiergarten*

An den S-Bahn-Bögen am Savignyplatz

Next to the elevated commuter railway on the *Savignyplatz*

Inlineskater im Tiergarten   Inline skaters in the *Tiergarten*

Das Shell-Haus am Landwehrkanal

The Shell building on the *Landwehrkanal*

Christopher Street Day am Kurfürstendamm

Christopher Street Day on the *Kurfürstendamm*

Bauhaus Archiv, Klingelhöferstraße, Tiergarten

Bauhaus archive, *Klingelhöferstrasse, Tiergarten*

Hutverkauf auf dem Kunstmarkt an der Spree hinter dem Zeughaus

Hat sales at the *Kunstmarkt* on the Spree behind the *Zeughaus*

vorhergehende Seite:
Zoologischer Garten, Elefantentor; rechts das Gebäude der Grundkreditbank

previous page:
Zoological garden, *Elefantentor* (Elephant Gate), on the right the *Grundkreditbank* building

Café am Winterfeldtplatz in Schöneberg

Café on the *Winterfeldtplatz* in *Schöneberg*

Der im Krieg beschädigte Turm der Kaiser-Wilhelm-Gedächtnis-kirche und das Kreuz des Anfang der sechziger Jahre gebauten Glockenturms

The tower of the Kaiser Wilhelm memorial church, damaged in the war, and the cross of the bell-tower, built in the early sixties

Ludwig-Erhard-Haus in der Fasanenstraße, Sitz der Berliner Börse und eines Dienstleistungszentrums der IHK; links daneben das alte Bürogebäude der IHK

Ludwig Erhard Haus in the *Fasanenstrasse*, seat of the Berlin stock exchange and of an *IHK* (Chamber of Industry and Commerce) service centre; adjoining, on left, the old *IHK* office building

In der Leibnizstraße in Charlottenburg

In the *Leibnizstrasse* in *Charlottenburg*

Paris Bar in der Kantstraße in Charlottenburg

Paris bar in the *Kantstrasse* in *Charlottenburg*

Bürohäuser der Klammt AG am Spreeufer in Moabit

Klammt company office buildings on the bank of the Spree in *Moabit*

Strandbad Wannsee   Bathing place on shore of *Wannsee*

Am Teufelssee   On the *Teufelssee*

vorhergehende Seite:
Der U-förmige Gebäudekomplex des Innenministeriums mit seinen Rundtürmen an der Spree in Moabit

previous page:
The U-shaped complex of buildings of the Ministry of Internal Affairs with its round towers on the Spree in *Moabit*

Inlineskater in der Trabantensiedlung Gropiusstadt

Inline skater in the satellite settlement of *Gropiusstadt*

U-Bahnhof Görlitzer Bahnhof   *Görlitzer Bahnhof* underground station

Deutsches Technikmuseum Berlin mit einer Douglas C-47, die während der Luftbrücke zum Einsatz kam (links); Trasse der U-Bahn-Linie 1 (rechts)

Deutsches Technikmuseum Berlin with a Douglas C-47, which was used during the airlift (left); underground track, line 1 (right)

Karneval der Kulturen in Kreuzberg

Karneval der Kulturen (Carnival of Cultures) in *Kreuzberg*

Berliner Abgeordnetenhaus (links) und Martin-Gropius-Bau (rechts) an der Niederkirchnerstraße in Mitte bzw. Kreuzberg

Berliner Abgeordnetenhaus (House of Parliament) (left) in Mitte and Martin Gropius building (right) on the Niederkirchnerstrasse in Kreuzberg

Ziergiebel des Eingangsportals vom ehemaligen Anhalter Bahnhof; durch den Kreisbogen ist im Hintergrund das Tempodrom sichtbar

Ornamental gable of the entrance portal of the former *Anhalter Bahnhof* railway station; through the circular arch the *Tempodrom* is visible in the background

Mauerreste am Lenné-Dreieck; links im Hintergrund die mittlerweile abgerissene Infobox am Potsdamer Platz

Wall ruins on the *Lenné-Dreieck;* in the background, left, the Infobox on the *Potsdamer Platz* which has since been torn down

Feuerwehrbrunnen am Mariannenplatz im Norden Kreuzbergs

Fire hydrant on the *Mariannenplatz* in the north of *Kreuzberg*

folgende Seite:
Blick vom Berliner Dom Richtung Osten; in der Bildmitte das Rote Rathaus, links der Fernsehturm

following page:
View from the *Berliner Dom* towards the east; in the middle of the picture the *Rotes Rathaus,* the television tower on left

Fans bei einem Auftritt der Kelly-Family vor dem Roten Rathaus

Fans at an appearance of the Kelly family at the *Rotes Rathaus*

Blick auf die Jungfernbrücke über den Spreekanal; links der westliche Spreearm um die Spreeinsel, rechts im Vordergrund ein 1898 erbautes Geschäftshaus mit neogotischer Fassade

View of the *Jungfernbrücke* over the Spree canal; on the left the western branch of the Spree flowing around the Spree island, in the foreground, right, a commercial building with neo-Gothic façade, built in 1898

Teilnehmer einer Veranstaltung zum Jesustag 2000 am Neptunbrunnen vor dem Roten Rathaus

Persons attending an event as part of the *Jesustag 2000*, at the *Neptunbrunnen* in front of the *Rotes Rathaus*

Blick über den Molkenmarkt in nördlicher Richtung; links das Nikolaiviertel mit der Nikolaikirche, in der Mitte das Rote Rathaus, daneben der Fernsehturm, rechts im Vordergrund der Kuppelturm des Alten Stadthauses

View over the Molkenmarkt to the north; on the left the Nikolai quarter with the *Nikolaikirche*, in the centre the *Rotes Rathaus*, with television tower adjacent, in foreground on right the cupola tower of the *Altes Stadthaus*

In der U-Bahn-Linie 1

On the underground, line 1

Bei einer Festveranstaltung zum Tag der Deutschen Einheit auf dem Pariser Platz

On a ceremonious occasion to mark the Day of German Unity on the *Pariser Platz*

vorhergehende Seite:
Gendarmenmarkt mit Deutschem Dom (links), Konzerthaus (Mitte) und Französischem Dom (rechts)

previous page:
Gendarmenmarkt with *Deutscher Dom* (left), concert hall (centre) and *Französischer Dom* (right)

In der Säulenvorhalle der Neuen Wache

In the pillared vestibule of the *Neue Wache*

Die Predigtkirche im Berliner Dom; rechts der Altarraum, links die Kaiserloge

The *Predigtkirche* in the *Berliner Dom*; on the right the altar precincts, on the left the Kaiser's box

Figurengruppe mit Krieger und der Göttin Athene auf der Schlossbrücke; im Hintergrund der Berliner Dom

Group of figures with warrior and the goddess Athena on the *Schlossbrücke*; in the background, the *Berliner Dom*

Eröffnungsfeier im Lichthof des Museums für Kommunikation Berlin in Mitte

Opening ceremony on the glass roofed courtyard of the *Museum für Kommunikation Berlin* in *Mitte*

Saal in der Alten Nationalgalerie, Marmorgruppe der Kronprinzessin Luise und ihrer Schwester Friederike von Johann Gottfried Schadow

Hall in the *Alte Nationalgalerie*, marble group by Johann Gottfried Schadow representing the Crown Princess Luise and her sister Friederike

Blick auf die nördliche Spitze der Museumsinsel mit dem Bode-Museum

View of the northern end of the *Museumsinsel* with the Bode Museum

Blick auf die Rückseite des Pergamonmuseums und der Alten Nationalgalerie aus nördlicher Richtung

View from the north of rear of the *Pergamonmuseum* and the *Alte Nationalgalerie*

Millenniumsausstellung 2000 im Hamburger Bahnhof (Museum für Gegenwart) in Tiergarten

Millennium exhibition, 2000, in the *Hamburger Bahnhof (Museum für Gegenwart)* in *Tiergarten*

Rosenthaler Straße mit den Hackeschen Höfen (links)

Rosenthaler Strasse with the Hackesche Höfe (left)

Innenhof der Kulturbrauerei in Prenzlauer Berg

Interior courtyard of the *Kulturbrauerei* in *Prenzlauer Berg*

Auf dem Kurfürstendamm beim ehemaligen Café Kranzler

On the *Kurfürstendamm* near the former *Café Kranzler*

Porträtmaler am Breitscheidplatz in Charlottenburg

Portait painter on the *Breitscheidplatz* in *Charlottenburg*

Blick in die Jägerstraße Richtung Gendarmenmarkt; rechts die spitzwinkligen Erker des Quartier 206, links die Galeries Lafayette, im Hintergrund der Turm des Französischen Doms

The *Jägerstrasse* looking towards the *Gendarmenmarkt*; on the right the angular bay windows of *Quartier 206*, on the left the *Galeries Lafayette*, in the background the tower of the *Französischer Dom*

Bahnhof Friedrichstraße   *Friedrichstrasse* railway station

Besucher im Jüdischen Museum in Kreuzberg

People visiting the *Jüdisches Museum* in *Kreuzberg*

Tanzgruppe im Tiergarten

Group of dancers in the *Tiergarten*

folgende Seite:
Die Spree in Berlins Mitte Richtung Norden; links das Haus der Deutschen Industrie, rechts das Nikolaiviertel

following page:
The Spree in centre of Berlin, looking north; on the left the *Haus der Deutschen Industrie* (House of German Industry), on the right the Nikolai quarter

Teilnehmer des Jesustages 2000 vor dem Berliner Dom

People attending the *Jesustag 2000* in front of the *Berliner Dom*

Tanzende Jugendliche vor dem Roten Rathaus

Young people dancing in front of the *Rotes Rathaus*

Oranienburger Straße mit den Kuppeln der Neuen Synagoge (links)

Oranienburger Strasse with the cupolas of the *Neue Synagoge* (left)

Dach des Museums für Kommunikation in Mitte mit der »Gigantengruppe«

Roof of the *Museum für Kommunikation* (Communications Museum) with group of giants, *Mitte*

Besuchergruppe vor dem ehemaligen DDR-Staatsratsgebäude am Schlossplatz; im Hintergrund rechts der Palast der Republik und der Berliner Dom

Group of visitors in front of the former GDR *Staatsrat* building on the *Schlossplatz*; in the background, right, the *Palast der Republik* and the *Berliner Dom*

Café am Hackeschen Markt   Café on the *Hackescher Markt*

Ernst-Thälmann-Denkmal im Ernst-Thälmann-Wohnpark an der Prenzlauer Allee

Ernst Thälmann monument in the Ernst Thälmann housing estate on the *Prenzlauer Allee*

Bauten der Karl-Marx-Allee am Frankfurter Tor in Friedrichshain

Buildings on the *Karl-Marx-Allee* by the *Frankfurter Tor* in *Friedrichshain*

Volkspark Rehberge in Wedding   Rehberge public park in *Wedding*

Der Märchenbrunnen im Volkspark Friedrichshain

Fairytale fountain in the *Friedrichshain* public park

U-Bahnhof Schlesisches Tor   *Schlesisches Tor* underground station

S-Bahnhof Ostkreuz　　*Ostkreuz* commuter railway station

Kneipe in der Gropiusstadt   Pub in *Gropiusstadt*

Multikulturelles Fest im Tiergarten   Multicultural festival in the *Tiergarten*

Oberbaumbrücke, Blick in Richtung Kreuzberg

Oberbaumbrücke, looking in the direction of *Kreuzberg*

Teilnehmer an einer Veranstaltung zum Tag der Deutschen Einheit auf dem Alexanderplatz

People attending an event to mark the Day of German Unity on the *Alexanderplatz*

Am Viktoria-Luise-Platz im Bayerischen Viertel, Schöneberg

On the *Viktoria-Luise-Platz* in the Bavarian quarter, *Schöneberg*

Bürokomplex »Trias« an der Holzmarktstraße in Mitte

Trias office complex on the *Holzmarktstrasse* in *Mitte*

Werk der GASAG in Mariendorf   *GASAG factory in Mariendorf*

Das Internationale Congress Centrum (ICC) in Charlottenburg, im Hintergrund der Funkturm

The International Congress Centre (ICC) in *Charlottenburg*, in the background the radio tower

folgende Seite:
Blick auf das Schloss Charlottenburg; die Stülerbauten im Vordergrund beherbergen die Sammlung Berggruen (links) und das Ägyptische Museum (rechts)

following page:
View of the *Schloss Charlottenburg*; the Stüler buildings in the foreground house the Berggruen collection (left) and the Egyptian Museum (right)

Blick vom Schloss Babelsberg auf Glienicker Brücke, Große Neugierde und Jagdschloss Glienicke (rechts)

View from the *Schloss Babelsberg* towards the *Glienicker Brücke*, *Große Neugierde* and Glienicke hunting lodge (right)

Die Sacrower Heilandskirche am Jungfernsee

The *Sacrow Heilandskirche* on the *Jungfernsee*

Das Kasino mit Pergola am Havelufer im Schlosspark Kleinglienicke

The casino with pergola on the bank of the Havel in the Kleinglienicke chateau grounds

folgende Seite:
Die Pfaueninsel in der Havel mit Schloss

following page:
The peacock island in the Havel with chateau

© 2003 Nicolaische Verlagsbuchhandlung GmbH, Berlin

Fotos:	Carl-Heinz Hatebur
Lektorat:	Diethelm Kaiser, Berlin
Übersetzung:	Theresa M. Bullinger, Berlin
Gestaltung:	Jonas Maron, Berlin
Satz und Repro:	Mega-Satz-Service, Berlin
Druck:	H. Heenemann, Berlin
Bindung:	Kunst- und Verlagsbuchbinderei Leipzig

Alle Rechte vorbehalten

ISBN 3-87584-965-5